Dedicated to Research

Dedicated to Research

Sagarika Datta

Library of Congress Control Number: 2022915259
ISBN: Hardcover   978-1-6698-3957-6
                   Softcover   978-1-6698-3959-0
                   eBook   978-1-6698-3958-3

Print information available on the last page.

Rev. date: 08/15/2022

To order additional copies of this book, contact:
Xlibris
844-714-8691
www.Xlibris.com
Orders@Xlibris.com
838166

CONTENTS

Acknowledgment

The pre-prints are taken from Research Square. Thanks to Research Square. Thanks to The International Council for Education of People with Visual Impairment and Webel Mediatronics Ltd. The published article(portion) in IEEE is taken from https://ieeexplore.ieee.org/

Role of Calcium Channel Blocker in Excessive Mast Cell Degranulation

Sagarika Datta

Abstract

Background:

I present a case of a female patient, age 45 years, for whom the uncontrolled mast cell degranulation created many issues related to allergy like, skin rash, itching, breathing discomfort, frequent throat infection, GERD, migraine, fibromyalgia, peripheral neuropathy, depression, anxiety disorder, constipation etc. For the patient, it was observed that calcium channel blockers seem to control the unnecessary and uncontrolled mast cell degranulation. CCB seemed to have a role to play in mast cell degranulation.

Case presentation:

When the patient is taking either Flunarizine or Pregabalin or both together, the need for antihistamine and montelukast are very low. The patient suffers less throat infection while Flunarizine or Pregabalin are being taken. More the dose of Pregabalin less the occurrence of any type of allergy (food, pollen, dust etc.). The requirement of corticosteroid inhaler for breathing discomfort is also less. Frequency of body pain, migraine is minimal. Occurrence of stomach acid or GERD or digestion disorder is also very less. In terms of mood or anxiety, body is stable too. So, per day when 3 Pregabalin (75mg) were taken with 1 Amitriptyline (50mg) and 1 Duloxetine (60mg) health is completely stable with no need for H1 Blocker, H2 Blocker, Montelukast and Corticosteroid inhaler.

Conclusion:

CCB, specifically L-type CCB must have role in controlling the degranulation of mast cells, thus reducing all problem together at the root. But there are disadvantages like aggravated IBS (lazy gut), aggravated RLS and fluid retention (swelling of palm).

We must check the use of Gabapentin and Sodium cromoglycate too. They should also control the unnecessary mast cell degranulation. Thus, fixing the problem at the root.

Figures:

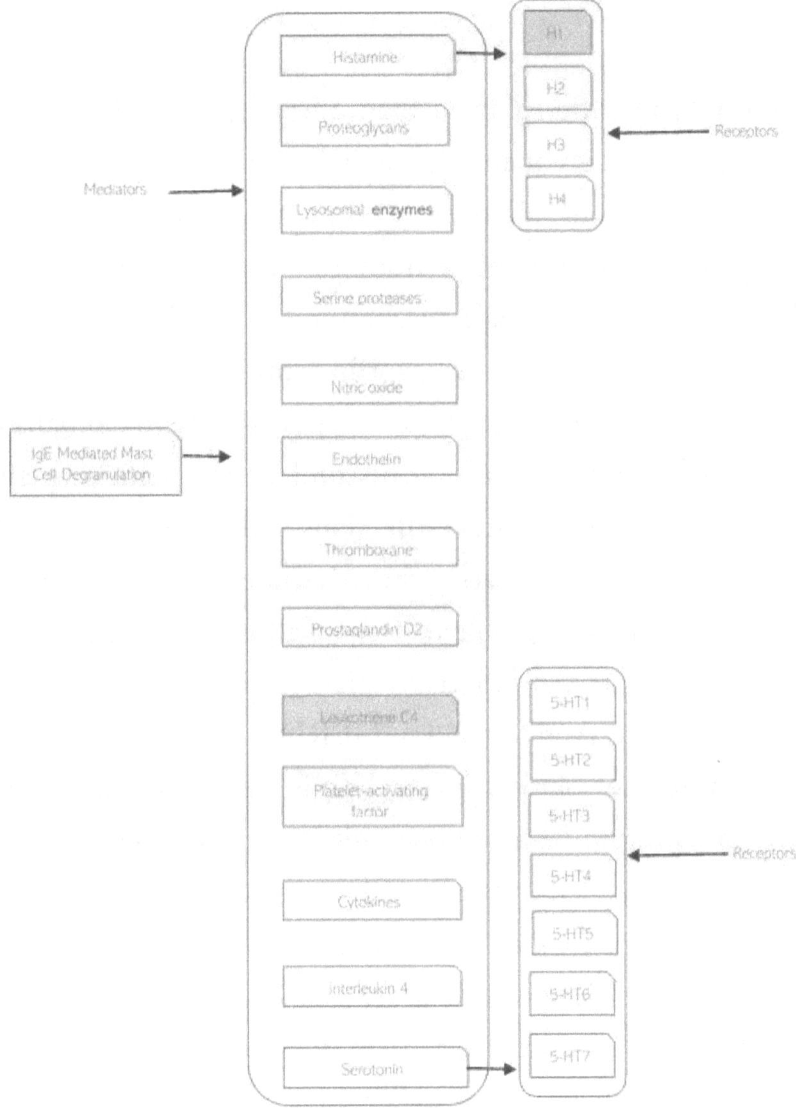

Mediators
IgE Mediated Mast Cell Degranulation
Histamine
Proteoglycans
Lysosomal enzymes
Serine proteases
Nitric oxide
Endothelin
Thromboxane
Prostaglandin D2
Leukotriene C4
Platelet-activating factor
Cytokines
Interleukin 4
Serotonin
Receptors
H1
H2
H3
H4
5-HT1
5-HT2
5-HT3
5-HT4
5-HT5
5-HT6
5-HT7
Receptors

Background:

Case:

The patient suffered from food allergy, pollen, dust, hot, cold allergy, and frequent throat infection from childhood. Due to continuous allergy and infection, patient started getting breathing discomfort from 12+ of age. Up to a time only antibiotics and cough syrups used to be the treatment procedure. After a certain time, antihistamine and montelukast tablets used to help for allergy and rashes, corticosteroid inhalers used to help for the breathing discomfort and azithromycin tablets used to help for throat infections. All these are for time being relief and not for treating the root cause. Later this patient grows, stomach acid problem, frequent headache, and body ache. Paracetamol and NSAID tablets helped controlling the pain temporarily. And for acid or GERD problem H2 blocker or PPI were the solution given. While the list of medicine started growing to be a big one, with age, new diseases also started getting added to the list. The headache and body ache became unbearable and more frequent, almost every day. So, migraine and fibromyalgia are added to the disease list. Patient was initially treated with Flunarizine. Migraine and food allergy problems were under control. It is known that Flunarizine is having some antihistamine properties. It has been seen that the patient was doing good when the medicine is applied. As soon as the medicine is stopped migraine and allergy both are back. At a given point, the patient started showing problems of anxiety disorder and neuropathy pain and more severe migraine. As a whole patient needed to deal with allergy, asthma, migraine, fibromyalgia, depression, GERD, RLS, weak muscle all problems together. H1 Blocker (SOS), H2 Blocker (SOS), Montelukast (SOS), Corticosteroid inhaler, Sertraline, Flunarizine, Pregabalin and NSAID (SOS) seemed to work to put the patient in a stable condition. After long term use of Sertraline, Flunarizine, Pregabalin patient started facing the problem of irritable bowel syndrome (IBS). Colonoscopy report shows, a lazy gut problem. This is probably due to the muscle relaxant medicines.

On using either Flunarizine or Pregabalin or both together, the need for antihistamine and montelukast are very low. The patient suffers less throat infection while Flunarizine or Pregabalin are being taken. More the dose of Pregabalin less the occurrence of any type of allergy (food, pollen, dust etc.). The requirement of corticosteroid inhaler for breathing discomfort is also less. Frequency of body pain, migraine is minimal. Occurrence of stomach acid or GERD or digestion disorder is also very less. In terms of mood or anxiety, body is stable too. So, per day when 3 Pregabalin (75mg) were taken with 1 Amitriptyline (50mg) and 1 Duloxetine (60mg) health is completely stable with no need for H1 Blocker, H2 Blocker, Montelukast and Corticosteroid inhaler.

The disadvantage is IBS is aggravated. Gut's motility is too low with all the muscle relaxants. There is difficulty peeing (Amitriptyline induced). More weight was gained (Pregabalin induced). There is problem of fluid retention. Palms were swelled. RLS frequency is increased with Pregabalin (3 times).

Discussion:

On using Flunarizine, it was previously seen that the need for H1 Blocker and H2 Blocker are much less. Later when patient is on Pregabalin the need for H1 Blocker and H2 Blocker are almost null. With Flunarizine no apparent disadvantages were seen but muscle pain was not controlled in a great deal. With Pregabalin allergy and related problems are almost gone but constipation, weight gain, fluid retention and RLS problems are reported. From a 15 to 20 years long observation, it seems that L-type calcium channel blocker has role to play in mast cell degranulation or in releasing histamine and other neurotransmitters which are responsible for all the discomforts in the patient. The advantage is restricting the release of histamine reducing allergy and breathing discomfort and restricting the release of glutamine in CNS thus reducing headaches. Amitriptyline too has some channel blocker features.

We must find out a way to consume selective calcium blockers controlling swelling and constipation.

Pregabalin along with Amitriptyline works excellent for all the above allergy related discomforts. Gabapentin and Sodium cromoglicate should also work fine. But this is not tested.

In Fig-1, it has been shown that, when unnecessary mast cell degranulation happens, then there are lot of mediators which can harm us (anything excessive is harmful for our body). As per the diagram, we can block only few of them. But if we stop the excessive degranulation, then the problem is fixed at root.

The unnecessary mast cell degranulation disturbs the intestine, and the released mediators start the problem of food allergy, food intolerance, IBS, and other problems. There may be one mediator that is responsible for disturbing the gut, or gut muscles become weaker, so the gut motility is affected. For food intolerance we see the problem starts after 4 to 12 hours later after eating. The Gut-brain axis is disturbed, results in gut disorder, and headache. One of the reasons of IBS can be excessive mast cell degranulation. But the mediator responsible is not yet identified.

So, it may not be too much of mast cell build up problem like mastocytosis, but moderate number of mast cell build up is the cause of too much sensitivity. Sodium cromoglycate medicine should be allowed for the treatment.

Somehow, the below medicine combination is helping in preventing too much of mast cell build up in few areas, or they are preventing the mast cell degranulation.

- Pregabalin (75mg) per day thrice
- Amitriptyline (50mg) per day one
- Duloxetine (60mg) per day one

We should also check the result when Pregabalin is replaced with Gabapentin or Sodium cromoglycate. Sodium cromoglycate is not available for treatment of IBS or other gut problems like food intolerance etc.

Declarations

Ethics approval and consent to participate: Not applicable

Consent for publication: Written informed consent was obtained from the patient for publication of this case report and any accompanying images. A copy of the written consent is available for review by the Editor-in-Chief of this journal

Availability of data and materials: Not applicable

Competing interest: None

Funding: No relevant funding to declare

Authors' contributions: DP: Contributed to writing the case and discussion, SR: Contributed to writing the case and discussion, JF: Contributed to writing the case and discussion, all authors have read and approved the final manuscript

Acknowledgements: Not applicable

Abbreviations

RLS: Restless Leg Syndrome
CNS: Central Nervous System
GERD: Gastroesophageal reflux disease
IBS: Irritable bowel syndrome
NSAID: Nonsteroidal anti-inflammatory drugs
CCB: Calcium Channel Blocker

References

https://en.wikipedia.org/wiki/L-type_calcium_channel
https://en.wikipedia.org/wiki/Flunarizine
https://en.wikipedia.org/wiki/Pregabalin
https://www.ncbi.nlm.nih.gov/pmc/articles/PMC3708031/
https://pubmed.ncbi.nlm.nih.gov/15241346/
https://en.wikipedia.org/wiki/Cromoglicic_acid
https://www.ncbi.nlm.nih.gov/pmc/articles/PMC3033552/

Addendum

This short communication (preprint) is published in research square on Jun 18, 2021. Later the article was published in International Journal of Medical and Biomedical Studies (IJMBS) on 2021-07-10.

Metabolic Acidosis & It's Connection with Other Diseases

Sagarika Datta

Abstract

After long observation and analysis, a connection between metabolic acidosis and migraine have been found in a female patient. She is suffering from headache from childhood. As, headache is not the primary cause it was difficult to treat. Several medicines worked when patient takes the medicine regularly. Headache is back when the drug is stopped. As the root cause was not found and not treated, there are several other problems started happening like muscle pain, weak muscle, numbness etc. Long-term metabolic acidosis has effect on the Gastroesophageal & Gastrointestinal motility. For the patient, it was observed that "Metabolic Acidosis" is the indicator. Acidosis takes place first.

There can be many reasons for metabolic acidosis, but with consistent disbalance of pH level in body it damages many areas of body. And there can be several diseases added to the list. Most importantly it interrupts the connection between CNS (Central nervous system) and ENS (Enteric nervous system). Due to this disconnection the signals coming from brain cannot reach the GI tract. Very few of the signals from (instruction to contract and relaxation of the GI tract) can reach. The fact is "Less signals, less motility" and the outcome is "lazy gut. There can exist false signals, wrong interpretations of the signals.

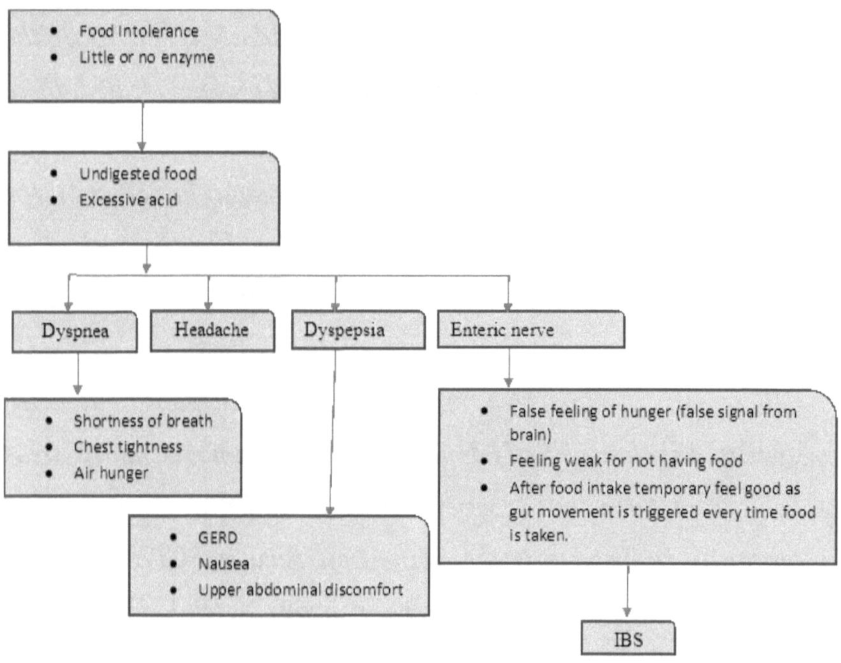

Food intolerance
Little or no enzyme

Undigested food
Excessive acid

Dyspnea
Headache
Dyspepsia
Enteric nerve

Shortness of breath
Chest tightness
Air hunger

GERD
Nausea
Upper abdominal discomfort

False feeling of hunger (false signal from brain)
Feeling weak for not having food
After food intake temporary feel good as gut movement is triggered every time food is taken.

IBS

For a female migraine patient, it has been observed that, headaches trigger after meals. We tried to maintain a history of food taken and were able to establish the below foods contributing to headache trigger,

List - 1

- Food that is causing allergic reaction like dairy (e.g., Milk and milk derivatives)
- Soy & soy products.
- Coconut, peanut & nut products.
- Meat.
- Food that is having flavor – Umami taste (e.g., Asafetida, Garlic, Fenugreek)
- Caffeine & caffeine derivatives.
- Seafood.
- Choco and chocolate product.
- Fermented food (Alcohol & beverages)
- Sesame seeds.
- Wheat.

Case Presentation

When treated with antihistamines, the patient showed improvement and less frequent episodes of headache. H1 blocker & H2 blockers are helpful but they cannot stop headaches. The use of calcium channel blockers was helpful. SSRI & SNRI drugs worked partially. But to fix the problem at root, gaining balance in the body's pH level is the most important task to do. Proton Pump Inhibitor category drugs were effective. Gaining back body's bicarbonate level is helpful.

Conclusion

Metabolic acidosis is the start and root cause of the several other problems like Migraine, Fibromyalgia, IBS, and muscle problems. Most of the problems are neurological, altered neurotransmitter release, disconnection between CNS & ENS. Body not being able to interpret efferent signals. There can be misinterpretation and false afferent signals.

The problem of "Metabolic Acidosis" can be hereditary.

Case

Beginning of the problem

The migraine trigger food list (List-1) is long. And if we carefully take a look at the list, we can see very little options are left for eating and fulfilling body's nutrition requirement. Quality of life becomes worse.

In the list most of the items are in "Food Intolerance" group. Few of them are in the "Food Allergy" group. Food intolerance signifies limited enzyme level. So, GI tract is the place where the problem is starting and then there is alteration of metabolism.

Metabolic acidosis is when the body produces too much of acid and body's pH level gets disbalanced. After long observation it was found that the patient is showing below symptoms along with the primary complaint of headache,

- Gas, acid, bloating, nausea.
- Muscle pain, stiffness in back neck.
- Weak muscle.
- Shortness of breath.
- Fast heart rate.
- Constipation.
- Low appetite.
- Mood swing.
- Anxiety & Depression.
- Food craving.
- Shivering, tremor sensation.

Discussion

Problem explanation & connection with acidosis:
Shortness of breath or Dyspnea, Fast heart rate

Carbon dioxide (CO_2) is a gas that is produced as a normal byproduct of our body's energy production. As per the normal body's process, CO_2 diffuses into bloodstream so that it can be exhaled from lungs. When CO_2 level become elevated, the signal reaches brain. Brain, then sends signal to the respiratory system to control CO_2 level, to decrease the level. Lung starts working heavily, it tries to exhale elevated CO_2. So, a deep and faster breathing continues until the oxygen & carbon dioxide levels are balanced again. When the signal reaches brain that

CO2 level is normal then the respiratory rate becomes normal again. If in the process of metabolism, CO2 production is more due to metabolic disorder then dyspnea is how the body tries to balance it. There is increase in heart rate too.

By the below equation we can see the process of glucose converting into CO2, H2O and energy,

$$C_6H_{12}O_6 + 6O_2 \rightarrow 6CO_2 + 6H_2O + energy$$

When the CO2 level increases, it gets diffused in red blood cells and the reaction is,

$$CO_2 + H_2O \rightarrow H_2CO_3 \rightarrow HCO_3^- + H^+$$

When H+ is increased, blood becomes acidic. The pH level decreases. To make it normal again, H+ level must come down or increased HCO3- level is required. When body's bicarbonate buffer is low, decreasing H+ level is the only solution otherwise we may provide HCO3- from external source. Respiratory chemoreceptors identify the CO2 level of blood and create signals (with the help of CNS) to take care of it.

Headache & it's connection with acidosis: (Migraine?)

It has been observed in the patient, from the pattern of her headache episodes, that the reason of the pain is due to excessive release of neuroexcitatory amino acids.

Histamine induced headache- For the patient, antihistamine drugs showed useful.

Glutamine induced headache-The umami taste is detected in mouth through the umami taste buds and the signal is sent to brain. These receptors are found in GI tract. Glutamate can bind with Umami receptors. This may trigger headache. Calcium channel blockers can prevent this condition.

Blood-Brain-Barrier is what protects the CNS from entering unwanted particles/substances.

From study, it has been established that carbon dioxide and lactic acid are discharged into the circulating cerebrospinal fluid. Thus, affecting the pH level of CNS. This triggers excitatory neurotransmitter release.

Mood, sleep, appetite, IBS & their connection with acidosis: (Lazy gut?)

Another important neurotransmitter to talk about is serotonin. 90% of it is produced in gut. It controls mood, sleep, appetite. It has role in digestion of food and gut motility. Undigested food in gut may create inflammation and prolonged inflammation may cause nerve cell deaths. This can limit the signals to the brain. This affects the bowel movement. Less signals from brain makes the gut lazy. On top of this, for the patient, as calcium channel blockers are taken for headache, that makes the gut lazier.

Central nervous system (CNS) & Enteric nervous system (ENS)

CNS & ENS always work in a synchronized manner. But for any nerve damage in gastrointestinal tract, this connection between CNS and ENS is lost or damaged, resulting in poor GI function including motility of gut.

Muscle weakness/pain & its connection with acidosis: (Fibromyalgia?)

Muscles contract when they receive signals from motor neurons. Due to damage in the nerve, there is less signals coming from motor neuron. Increased H+ level triggers muscle pain.

Tremor & it's connection with acidosis:

The patient occasionally faces the episodes of tremor or shivering of whole body.

Papilledema & it's connection with acidosis:

Papilledema is also seen in the patient during the episodes of headache.

Abbreviations

END	Enteric Nervous System
CNS	Central Nervous System
GERD	Gastroesophageal reflux disease
IBS	Irritable bowel syndrome

Declarations

Ethics approval and consent to participate: Not applicable

Consent for publication: Written informed consent was obtained from the patient for publication of this case report and any accompanying images. A copy of the written consent is available for review by the Editor-in-Chief of this journal

Availability of data and materials: Not applicable
Competing interest: None
Funding: No relevant funding to declare
Authors' contributions:
DP: Contributed to writing the case and discussion,
SR: Contributed to writing the case and discussion,
JF: Contributed to writing the case and discussion, all authors have read and approved the final manuscript
Acknowledgements: Not applicable

References

https://www.sciencedirect.com/topics/biochemistry-genetics-and-molecular-biology/amino-acid-metabolism
https://pubmed.ncbi.nlm.nih.gov/31272187/
https://en.wikipedia.org/wiki/Plasma_protein_binding
https://pubmed.ncbi.nlm.nih.gov/8092567/
https://www.sciencedirect.com/topics/nursing-and-health-professions/acidosis
https://fluidsbarrierscns.biomedcentral.com/articles/10.1186/s12987-019-0128-7
https://www.ncbi.nlm.nih.gov/pmc/articles/PMC2613646/

Addendum

This short communication (preprint) is published in research square on Nov 16, 2021. Later the article was published in www.imedpub.com Journal of Emergency and Trauma Care.

Effectivity of Flunarizine in Controlling Acidosis Induced Headache

Sagarika Datta

Abstract
Background:

In my previous case report, I mentioned about the connection between metabolic acidosis and other diseases. Headache is one of the diseases mentioned in a female patient. For the patient, it was observed that acidosis is the indicator. Acidosis takes place first.

There can be many reasons for metabolic acidosis.

For this patient it was seen that, food is the trigger. With consistent disbalance in pH level in body it exhibits many symptoms like palpitations, altered mental status such as severe anxiety due to hypoxia, nausea, abdominal pain, altered appetite and weight gain, muscle weakness, bone pain, and joint pain.

In acidosis the arterial carbon dioxide tension increases, and it can cross the blood-brain barrier and changes extravascular pH. Headache is trigger.

Patient was treated with Pregabalin, Amitriptyline and Duloxetine combination.

Frequency of headache was less but it was not stopped. Then patient was treated with CGRP receptor blocker subcutaneous injection but was not able to get rid of the throbbing head pain.

On using Flunarizine (Sibelium 10 mg) the headache was stopped on 2 days of medicine taking. It helped in reducing allergy-like symptoms too.

The effectivity of Flunarizine in controlling acidosis related headache is well proved.

Conclusion:

CCB, specifically L-type CCB must have role in controlling the degranulation of mast cells, thus reducing all problem together at the root. But there are disadvantages like aggravated IBS (lazy gut), aggravated RLS and fluid retention (swelling of palm).

We must check the use of Gabapentin and Sodium cromoglycate too. They should also control the unnecessary mast cell degranulation. Thus, fixing the problem at the root.

Figures:

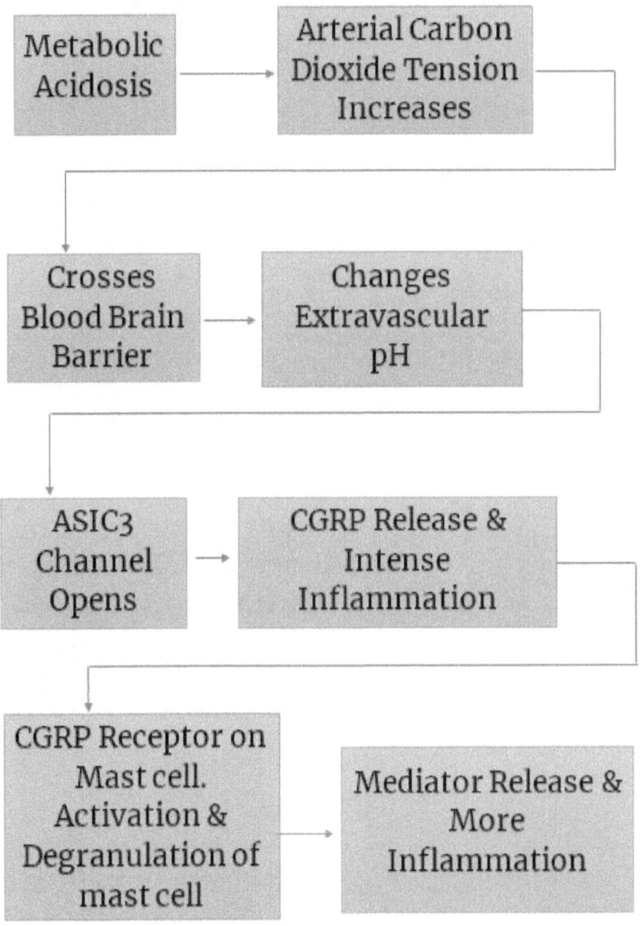

Figure - 1

Let us identify the ways to stop migraine trigger

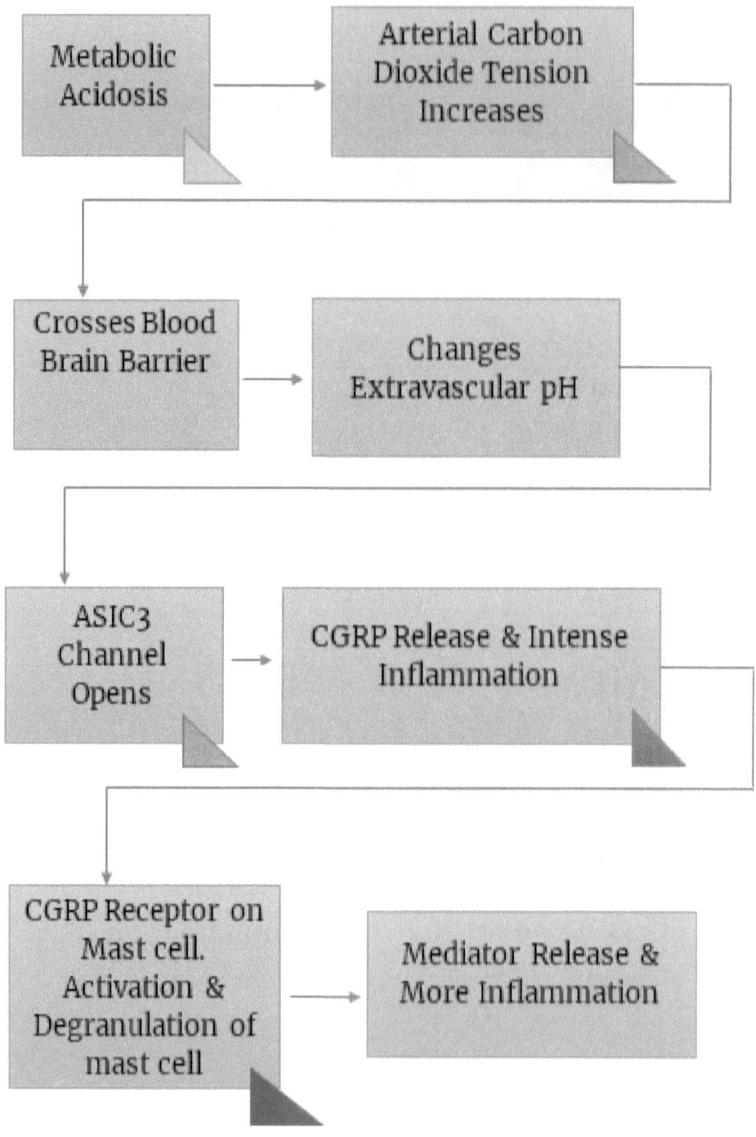

Figure – 2

To get rid of acute headache
Electrolytes, Decreasing CO_2 Tension
Increase Bicarbonate Level (Carbonated Water)
ASIC3 Channel Inhibitor
CGRP Receptor Inhibitor, CCB
H1 Receptor Inhibitor, CCB
Pain already triggered, Painkiller

Figure – 3

Root cause
Acidosis
Disbalance in CNS pH
Medicine that does not allow to open channel
ASIC3 channel open
CGRPR Blocker
5-HT1B receptor, 5-HT1D receptor
Intense inflammation & more neuro peptide release
CGRP release
H1 receptor blocker
Mast cell degranulation & mediator release

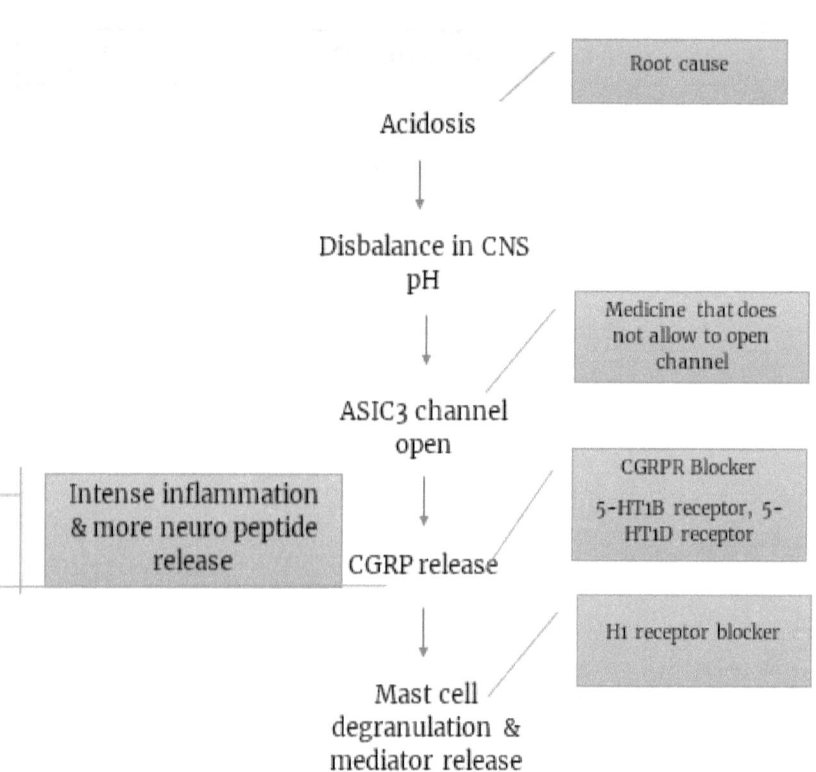

Figure – 4

Background:
Case:

Metabolic acidosis happens when,

Body's acid production increases

Kidney not being able to excrete enough acid.

Bicarbonate loss.

Body's bicarbonate buffer is low.

After long observation it was found that the patient is showing below symptoms along with the primary complaint of headache,

1. Gas, acid, bloating, nausea.
2. Muscle pain, stiffness in back neck.
3. Weak muscle.
4. Shortness of breath.
5. Fast heart rate.
6. Constipation.
7. Low appetite.
8. Mood swing.
9. Anxiety & Depression.
10. Food craving.
11. Shivering, tremor sensation.

Case Presentation

Carbon dioxide (CO_2) is a gas that is produced as a normal by-product of our body's energy production. As per the normal body's process, CO2 diffuses into bloodstream so that it can be exhaled from lungs. When CO2 level become elevated, the signal reaches brain. Brain, then sends signal to the respiratory system to control CO2 level, to decrease the level. Lung starts working heavily, it tries to exhale elevated CO2. So, a deep and faster breathing continues until the oxygen & carbon dioxide levels are balanced again.

In acidosis the arterial carbon dioxide tension increases, and it can cross the blood-brain barrier and changes extravascular pH. This imbalances pH level of CNS. Blood vessels get dilated. This triggers excitatory neurotransmitter release.

Once released, they travel to the outer layer of brain, the meninges. Which results in inflammation and swelling of blood vessels, causing an increase in blood flow around the brain. This makes the inflammation of the blood vessels resulting in throbbing pain.

Patient was initially treated with Pregabalin, Amitriptyline and duloxetine combination. The combination worked for some time, but headache was not stopped completely, only the frequency was less.

Patient took Ibuprofen (600mg) in SoS basis.

Later patient was given Aimovig (CGRP receptor inhibitor) subcutaneous injection. After taking the injection patient was able to be without headache for 7 consecutive days but after that headache again started.

Unavailability of Flunarizine in the locality was the cause patient was not able to take flunarizine.

Once started with Flunarizine (Sibelium 10mg) patient was

able to get rid of the headache. This implies Flunarizine has the capability to decrease carbon dioxide tension in CNS.

On using either Flunarizine or Pregabalin or both together, the need for antihistamine and montelukast are very low. The patient suffers less throat infection while Flunarizine or Pregabalin are being taken. More the dose of Pregabalin less the occurrence of any type of allergy (food, pollen, dust etc.). The requirement of corticosteroid inhaler for breathing discomfort is also less. Frequency of body pain, migraine is minimal. Occurrence of stomach acid or GERD or digestion disorder is also very less. In terms of mood or anxiety, body is stable too. So, per day when 3 Pregabalin (75mg) were taken with 1 Amitriptyline (50mg) and 1 Duloxetine (60mg) health is completely stable with no need for H1 Blocker, H2 Blocker, Montelukast and Corticosteroid inhaler.

The disadvantage is IBS is aggravated. Gut's motility is too low with all the muscle relaxants. There is difficulty peeing (Amitriptyline induced). More weight was gained (Pregabalin induced). There is problem of fluid retention. Palms were swelled. RLS frequency is increased with Pregabalin (3 times).

Discussion:

<u>Pregabalin</u> works as a selective calcium channel blocker (CCB). This medication is used to treat neuropathic pain, fibromyalgia, restless leg syndrome, and generalized anxiety disorder.

<u>Amitriptyline</u> inhibits serotonin transporter (SERT) and

norepinephrine transporter (NET). Amitriptyline additionally acts as a potent inhibitor of the serotonin 5-HT2A, 5-HT2C, the α1A-adrenergic, the histamine H1. It is a non-selective blocker of multiple ion channels voltage-gated sodium channels.

Duloxetine is used to treat fibromyalgia, and neuropathic pain. It is a serotonin–norepinephrine reuptake inhibitor.

Erenumab targets the calcitonin gene-related peptide receptor (CGRPR) for the prevention of migraine.

Flunarizine is a selective calcium antagonist. Other actions include,

- Antihistamine
- Serotonin receptor blocking
- Dopamine D2 blocking activity.
- It has been theorized that it may act not by inhibiting calcium entry into cells, but rather by an intracellular mechanism such as antagonizing calmodulin.
- It readily passes the blood–brain barrier.

In research, it has been found that flunarizine can decrease the carbon dioxide tension in CNS. So, for acidosis induced headaches, flunarizine is the best.

As flunarizine has antihistamine property, it should be able to stop allergy induced headaches.

It has been observed in the patient that, calcium channel blocker drugs help in reducing symptoms of allergy.

It may happen that CCB drugs restrict the degranulation of the mast cells.

Now, to get rid of allergy there are two ways,

1. Drug that inhibits histamine H1 receptor. In that case the other mediators' receptors are not inhibited. And it is not possible to restrict downstream action of all mediators.
2. Stopping the unnecessary degranulation of mast cells.

Pregabalin can help in reducing the mast cell granulations. So, it contributes to allergy induced acute headaches. That is why use of pregabalin can lower the acute headache frequency.

Amitriptyline has the property of several receptor blocker. This helps to inhibit the receptors when the degranulation has already taken place, and mediators are playing and contributing to acute headache trigger.

That is why the combination of medicines Pregabalin, and Amitriptyline can lower the frequency of acute headache but cannot stop them.

It has been seen that during migraine headache CGRP, calcitonin gene-related peptide is released around the brain. When CGRP is released, it causes intense inflammation in the coverings of the brain (the meninges) and starts the headache. CGRP also contribute to linger the headache up to several hours.

The next question comes, why does CGRP release take place in brain?

Let us draw a sequence diagram.

Let us identify the ways to stop migraine trigger

CGRP receptor blocking is the 4th Layer. Flunarizine (Sibelium) may have the property of decreasing CO_2 tension in CNS. That is how it controls opening the ASIC3 channels. So, CGRP is not released, and no mast cell degranulation happens. As a result, no histamine release.

Conclusion

From the discussion flunarizine is very effective in acidosis induced acute headaches. We have seen that the other medicines are not working at the root cause level.

Declarations

Ethics approval and consent to participate: Not applicable

Consent for publication: Written informed consent was obtained from the patient for publication of this case report and any accompanying images. A copy of the written consent is available for review by the Editor-in-Chief of this journal

Availability of data and materials: Not applicable

Competing interest: None

Funding: No relevant funding to declare

Authors' contributions: DP: Contributed to writing the case and discussion, SR: Contributed to writing the case and discussion, JF: Contributed to writing the case and discussion, all authors have read and approved the final manuscript

Acknowledgements: Not applicable

Abbreviations

CGRP	Calcitonin gene-related peptide
CNS	Central Nervous System
ASIC3	Acid Sensing Ion Channel 3
CCB	Calcium Channel blocker

References

https://www.researchsquare.com/article/rs-1083755/v1
https://en.wikipedia.org/wiki/Metabolic_acidosis
https://pubmed.ncbi.nlm.nih.gov/11903546/
https://en.wikipedia.org/wiki/Flunarizine
https://en.wikipedia.org/wiki/Amitriptyline
https://en.wikipedia.org/wiki/Duloxetine
https://en.wikipedia.org/wiki/Erenumab
https://pubmed.ncbi.nlm.nih.gov/19796656/
https://www.ncbi.nlm.nih.gov/pmc/articles/PMC4458434/
https://www.researchgate.net/figure/Proton-stimulation-of-calcitonin-gene-related-peptide-CGRP-secretion-involves_fig4_232698549
https://www.ncbi.nlm.nih.gov/pmc/articles/PMC1308857/
https://link.springer.com/article/10.1007/s13311-018-0619-2
https://en.wikipedia.org/wiki/Calcitonin_gene-related_peptide
https://www.youtube.com/watch?v=bvS646hm5v8

MATHEMATICS BRAILLE

M.N.G. Mani, ICEVI and S.N. Goswami, Shashanka J. Dutta, Sagarika Datta

Abstract

Editors that can convert English text to Braille and conversely Braille to English text have been around for decades, similarly we have text editors to convert Mathematical symbols like Square Root, Integration, and Statistical symbols. But what we don't have is an integrated application interface that supports these functions simultaneously, allowing users to compose mathematical? Text in a user? Friendly format and subsequently convert it into Braille. We propose a system to achieve this. Research on 'Writing Mathematical symbols alongside? text' is still ongoing. We plan to develop a system that will enable users to express in braille any mathematical statement linearly. Braille is entered and edited using six keys as it would be on a mechanical braille writer. The editor includes all the common features of a normal editor like copying, pasting, saving files, opening files etc.

Introduction

Our objective is to design a system for publishing Mathematics and Science books in Braille. Using this software, teachers and transcribers can produce relatively simply braille documents for Mathematics and science subjects.

Braille Code & Nemeth Braille Code

Braille is a code, which enables blind persons to read and

write. It was invented by a blind Frenchman, Louis Braille, in 1829. Braille is embossed by hand (or with a machine) onto thick paper and read with the fingers moving across on top of the dots. Braille's basic building block is a rectangular 3x2 six-dot cell, which provides 63 possible combinations representing print letters and symbols. Braille characters take up three times as much space as print. The basic Braille symbol (or cell) is composed of six dots arranged in two vertical columns, each column being three dots high. These dots are numbered as follows:

$$1 \circ \circ 4$$
$$2 \circ \circ 5$$
$$3 \circ \circ 6$$

Because this pattern produces only 63 one-cell symbols (plus the blank cell, which is used as a space), some symbols have multiple meanings, and many symbols which take only one character in print require more than one cell in Braille.

The Nemeth Braille Code for Mathematics and Science Notation is used (obviously) for mathematics and science material, which contains symbols not available in Literary Braille.

The Nemeth Code is not simply an expanded version of the Literary Braille Code; there are many significant differences. For example, numerals and some symbols (such as the dollar sign) are written differently and some Literary Code contractions cannot be used under certain circumstances. The codebook,

The Nemeth Code for Mathematics and Science Notation, 1972 Revision, lists 40 pages of symbols, each page containing between 12 and 21 symbols.

1 2 3 4 5 6 7 8 9 0

Fig: Nemeth Numerals

Text To Braille

Text to Braille conversion is most commonly through the use of ASCII characters using a one–to-one correspondence. Since our system needs to include English characters, Braille and Mathematical symbols simultaneously we need a wide range of characters and therefore our chosen format is the16-bit Unicode format rather than the simpler 8-bit ASCII format.

A B C D E F G H I J

K L M N O P Q R S T

U V X Y Z & = (!)

* < % ? : $] \ [W

1 2 3 4 5 6 7 8 9 0

/ + # > ' -

@ ^ _ + , ; '

Fig: Braille ASCII Chart

Linear representation of Mathematical Statements

The problem of encoding mathematics for computer processing or electronic communication is longstanding. For many years ASCII was the standard method of formatting mathematical and scientific text, but it was difficult to represent complex statements in ASCII, and in 1986 TeX was adopted as a mark-up method for mathematics.

Writing Mathematical symbols with keyboard and getting the saved version of the content is not complicated presently. Because so many work have been developed till now. As for example we can say about Microsoft Word's Equation Editor. And the software is pretty good. It can insert an equation as an object and edit using the many buttons provided. It is now relatively easy to produce complex mathematical formulae in print using programs such as Microsoft Word's Equation Editor, but these do not readily convert into braille. When we prepare a file containing English text and Mathematical symbols in print?, in most cases the mathematical statements are inserted as a part of a picture which software designers refer to as an "object". The following figure depicts an "object" representing a Pythagorean Theorem. It is virtually impossible to convert it electronically into braille.

$$\text{pythagorean theorem}$$

$$r = -b \pm \frac{\sqrt{b^2 - 4ac}}{2a}$$

Fig: equation inserted using MS's Equation editor.

Another common approach to producing mathematic and scientific text in print is to use? the computer language MathML. MathML is an XML application for describing mathematical notation and capturing both its structure and content. The goal of MathML is to enable mathematics to be served, received, and processed on the Web, just as HTML has enabled this functionality for text. MathML can be used to encode both mathematical notation and mathematical content. A small example is given here to show the use of MathML. We have to write the following MathML code to express (a + b)2. One form of presentation markup for this example is:

```
<msup>
<mfenced>
<mrow>
<mi>a</mi>
<mo>+</mo>
<mi>b</mi>
</mrow>
</mfenced>
<mn>2</mn>
</msup>
```

The content markup for the same example is:

```
<apply>
<power/>
<apply>
<plus/>
<ci>a</ci>
<ci>b</ci>
</apply>
<cn>2</cn>
</apply>
```

In its current form it does not convert to Braille since Braille conversion requires mathematical text to be presented in a linear form. For example, a linear representation of the statement (a+b)2 might take the form (a+b)<super>2, similarly Logex could be represented as Log<sub>e<val>x.

The codes inside the <> signs are the tags that represent a statement. The principle of the system we are proposing for representing mathematical and scientific formulae is to begin from the Braille and to use Rich Text Format (RTF) – an editing format that automatically saves data in a linear form.

The codes inside <> sign are the tags to represent a statement. We do not use any conventional way for linear representation rather we find what the Braille representation of it and go forward accordingly. So we do not face problems in representing simple fraction, complex fraction, mixed fraction and so on.

Rich Text Format (RTF) is a format that saves data in a linear form. So, we choose RTF as our editor format.

Rich Text Format

The Rich Text Format (RTF) Specification provides a format for text and graphics interchange that can be used with different output devices, operating environments, and operating systems. RTF uses the American National Standards Institute (ANSI), PC-8, Macintosh, or IBM PC character set to control the representation and formatting of a document, both on the screen and in print. With the RTF Specification, documents created under different operating systems and with different software applications can be transferred between those operating systems and applications. There is a header part and a data part. Data part it stores is nothing but the linear representation of what is written. As for example if you write the expression (a+b)2=a2+b2+2ab, as a header? RTF will hold the following information for it.

(a+b)\super 2\nosupersub =a\super 2\nosupersub +b\super 2\nosupersub +2ab

So, it is really helpful for us to use Rich Text Format.

Braille conversion:

We already said that we are using point-to-point mechanism for Braille conversion. Here is an example of the above statement to show the conversion procedure.

Displayed code: (a+b)2=a2+b2+2ab

Linear code: (a+b)\super 2\nosupersub =a\super 2\nosupersub +b\super 2\nosupersub +2ab

Braille code:

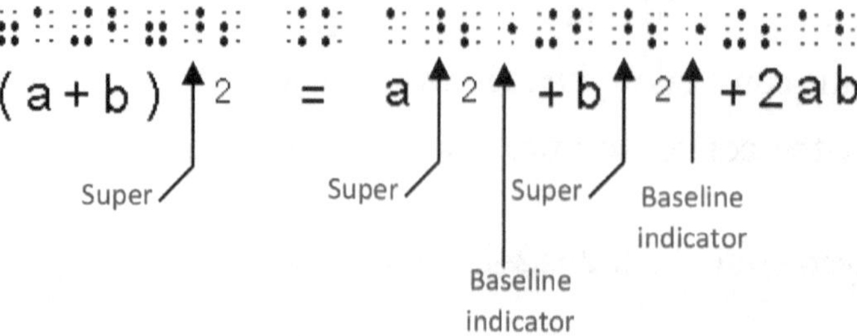

Fractions

Fractions in Braille can be represented both spatially and linearly. It is usually easier for a visually impaired person to read them linearly although it becomes difficult to understand spatial representations of large expressions like complex and hyper complex fractions through this method. Expressions like integrals and summations are also usually represented in linear form. For our purposes we have adopted a linear presentation approach for fractions e.g. (1/2+3/4)/(1/3+2/3).

Editing in Braille

If required we can edit the converted code using six keys on the keyboard S, D, F, J, K and L each representing a dot in the basic braille cell. Using these six keys we can get all the combinations for single cell Braille signs.

S - dot 3
D - dot 2
F - dot 1

J - dot 4

K - dot 5

L - dot 6

We can define two states for each key '0' and '1'. A pressed, key represents "1" but unpressed it represents 0. This is the format of the binary string that will be formed after each stroke.

E.g., if only F key is pressed, and rest are left then the corresponding string will be 00000001. We define a hash-table to get all combinations of the Braille codes. Here is a small part of the hash-table.

Key Combination	Braille code
00000000	10240 ⠀
00000001	10241 ⠁
00000010	10242 ⠂
00000011	10243 ⠃
00000100	10244 ⠄
00000101	10245 ⠅
00000110	10246 ⠆

Mathematics Braille Editor Interface and Language Selection

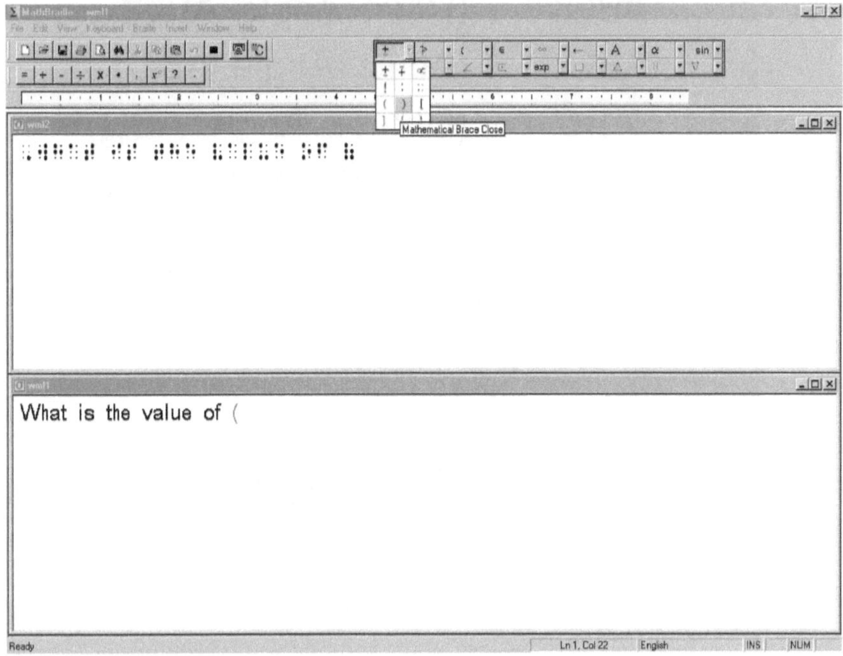

Fig: Math Editor Interface

To select the language of your choice, click on the Language select pop up on the Status Bar. Default Language is English. Clicking left mouse button when English language is selected will change it to Six Keys mode. Click again to come back to English.

Results and Discussion

Here is an example file that is composed in our system along with the converted Braille file, is given.

(1) ∠ ABC   (Angle ABC)
(2) ∟ ABC   (Right Angle ABC)
(3) ∠ ABC   (Acute Angle ABC)
(4) ∠ ABC   (Obtuse Angle ABC)
(5) ∠ ABC   (Straight Angle ABC)

Discussions:

This is the one and only one editor that supports simultaneous occurrence of writing and converting exists. Converted Braille file is editable using six keys in Braille. Mathematics Toolbar is available for inserting symbols. Conversion to Braille is done as per Nemeth Braille standard. It provides the facility to take normal print and also Braille print. Embossing through Index Interpoint Braillers is possible from here. The system has some errors in Braille conversion. As there is a number of rules for

Braille conversion, the process of incorporating new rules are also going on.

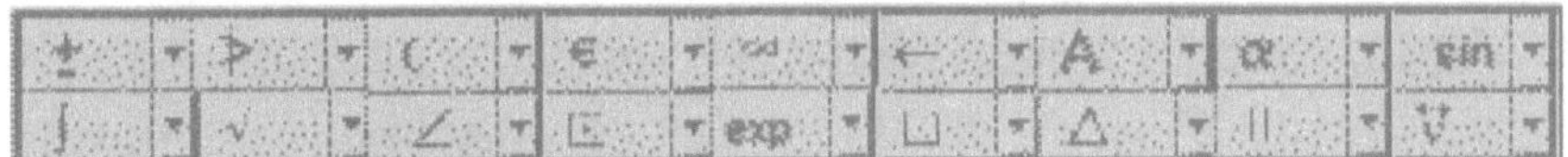

Fig: Mathematics Toolbar

References:

1. Nemeth Code for Mathematics and Science, 1972, American Association of the Workers for the blind, Association for education of the visually impaired and National Braille Association

2. www.w3.org/TR/MathML2.htm for MathML specification

Addendum

This article was published in the "Tech Talk" section of The Educator – January 2006. ICEVI has consultative status with the UN Economic and Social Council. ICEVI is a founding member of the UNICEF NGO Committee on Children with Disabilities, and they also work closely with UNESCO, The World Bank, and the World Health Organization. ICEVI works closely with national and civil society organizations concerned with education, as well as organizations of parents and persons with disabilities.

Unlike the first three short communications, this one is on developing a computer editor program that will help visually impaired people to scan a paper and let that program be executed and convert the text on the paper to Braille equivalent. This Braille editor was supporting multiple Indian languages. The editor was not only supporting Indian languages but mathematical signs and symbols, complex equation everything.

Segmentation of Bangla Unconstrained Handwritten Text

U. Pal and Sagarika Datta Computer Vision and Pattern Recognition Unit Indian Statistical Institute, 203 B. T. Road, Kolkata-108, India Email: umapada@isical.ac.in

Abstract

To take care of variability involved in the writing style of different individuals in this paper we propose a robust scheme to segment unconstrained handwritten Bangla texts into lines, words, and characters. For line segmentation, at first, we divide the text into vertical stripes. Stripe width of a document is computed by statistical analysis of the text height in the document. Next, we determine horizontal histogram of these stripes and the relationship of the minimal values of the histograms is used to segment text lines. Based on vertical projection profile lines are segmented into words. Segmentation of characters from handwritten word is very tricky as the characters are seldom vertically separable. We use a concept based on water reservoir principle for the purpose. Here we, at first, identify isolated and connected (touching) characters in a word. Next touching characters of the word are segmented based on the reservoir base area points and structural feature of the component.

Introduction

Segmentation of unconstrained handwritten text line is difficult because of inter-line distance variability and base-line skew variability. Components of two consecutive text-lines may be touched or overlapped in unconstrained handwritten text. These overlapping or touching characters complicate the line segmentation task greatly. In Bangla touching or overlapping occurs frequently because of modified characters of upper-zone and lower-zone (modified characters, upper-zone and lower-zone are described later). Many techniques (for example, global and partial projection analysis [9], techniques based on statistical modeling [6], etc.) are used for text line segmentation from non-Indian scripts. There is no work on hand-written text line segmentation of Indian scripts. Most of the characters in Bangla handwritten words are touching and segmentation of touching characters is the main bottleneck in handwritten recognition system. Many techniques have been proposed on touching character segmentation [3]. One class of approaches uses contour features of the component for segmentation [4]. Some researchers use profile features for touching character segmentation. Thinning based methods are also reported for touching characters segmentation [5]. Combined features-based methods are also used for the touching string segmentation [7]. Although many methods on handwritten line, word and character segmentation have been published in the literature for Roman, Chinese, Japanese, and Arabic scripts [3] only one report is available on character segmentation from Bangla handwritten isolated words[2]. They used recursive contour following technique for character segmentation from a word. In this paper we propose a robust scheme to segment handwritten texts of Bangla script into lines, words, and characters. Bangla is the second-most popular language in the Indian sub-continent and fifth-most popular language in the world. For line segmentation we divide the text into vertical stripes and determine horizontal histogram projections of these stripes. The relationship of the minimal values of the histograms is used to segment text lines. Based on vertical projection profile, lines are segmented into words. Segmentation of characters from handwritten word is difficult as the characters are mostly connected in a word. For character segmentation we first detect isolated and touching characters in a word. Touching characters of the word are then segmented based on the feature obtained from water reservoir concept [8].

Note: The full-length article is not provided here.

Addendum

Published in: Seventh International Conference on Document Analysis and Recognition, 2003. Proceedings.

Date of Conference: 06-06 August 2003
Date Added to IEEE Xplore: 08 September 2003
Print ISBN:0-7695-1960-1

9 781669 839590